Nathan Coppedge

Psychology

By Nathan Coppedge

Nathan Coppedge

ABSTRACT

A famous psychologist once said: "Money and sandwiches: the key to man and woman."
This text begins with four exceptional chapters: (Exceptional Psychology, Expressionist Psychology, Multi-Mind, and Brokenality), the author sets out to boldly explore the nuances of function and dysfunction, optimism, and madness. A bold narrative in the tradition of Jungian psychology. Recommended for those studying functionalism, behavioral therapy, cognition, and schizophrenia. The author has experience with mental illness, and is the previous author of numerous psychological texts.

Exceptional Psychology

Initially, I began with the concept of 'meaningful' psychology. True, this term has been plagued by a long tradition of pessimism and the symptoms that belie it. Not just the depressive avoidance of meaning, but also the schizophrenic annihilation of what normal people consider meaningful.

Next, I interpreted meaningful psychology through the lens of positive thinking. True, not all behaviors and psychological events have positive meaning, as Jung pointed out. However, the positive does have a potential for positive analysis (just as it has potential for positive everything else). So, not just positive, but meaningful positive interpretation seemed to be a particular course towards if nothing else, then at least discovering within the psychological experience what the patient wants to find. That in itself seemed like a significant principle.

Then, afterwards, I set out to find principles which would establish the significance of this positive psychology for the therapist. True, I was not a professional psychologist. But I had learned a few things about medicine and intellect in general, and I was eager to apply them.

My conclusion of this investigation was that positive psychology was about the significance of the patient, not simply as client or creator of psychological events, but as specifically the creator of meaningful psychological events. And not just meaningful psychological events, but as creator of any kind of meaningful event, in fact any kind of positive meaning.

(Clearly negative psychological events could be treated as expressive of disease, so positive psychological events could be seen as symptomatic of a lack of disease. This itself was a promising principle.)

If you look in the section under the Nature of Meaning, you will find some suggestions on the creation of meaningful experiences, and the types and varieties of significance that may be possible. An additional criterion of meaningful or exceptional psychology may be: 1. To leave topics open to criticism, 2. To affirm the positive and meaningful aspects of the client's critiques, 3. To provide physical reassurance of the existence of significance itself, depending on the client's specific interests, and 4. To promote functional concepts of life development and behavior qua meaning, watching for early warning signs of delusion, disillusionment, mental stress, and boredom.

Expressionist Psychology

After working on my thoughts about exceptional psychology I came to the conclusion that it was in itself not a complete approach. It did not address the exact, exact technique for therapy. It was, in a sense, ignorant of the genuine therapeutic process. Although this may be stating it in harsh terms (I did think that exceptional psychology was an important discovery), I also felt that in some ways, exceptional psychology was merely information psychology, that it didn't offer enough bells and whistles at least as I had developed it. Some clients may come away from significant therapy thinking that therapy was all the world had to offer, or that all the world had been offered to them, and it wasn't much

So, I set about finding a second concept of therapy. The tools this time involved for one thing an idea of a happy place of psychology. Therapy was an attachment to thaat happy place, and other activities could be attachments to other happy places. The scene of urban life is a series or lattice of happy places all strung together. The theory is people will not know to be happy unless they're told. It is never about how, it is only about what. Secondly, anything related to these experiences is an opportunity to get something from happiness, or to make happiness happier. Happiness only works with a happy theory, so everything that is given to happiness produces more happiness. Likewise, everything taken from happiness is obviously happy, because happiness is a happy place. Finally, the important part is that happiness is not just one theory. Anything functional and emotional is a kind of happiness, and many forms of this emotion are not just happy, but highly interesting and complex. We are to understand on one level, that happiness is what emotions are. And on another level, happiness is just a basic lesson of therapy. We are free to move beyond therapy and be very functional people, if we just remember that emotions are happy. That is the basic lesson.

Multi-Mind

After I was finished with Expressionist Psychology I looked for a further theory which would explain the worst mental cases. Maybe some people had unavoidable negative experiences. That was one thought. Perhaps what was bad about some experiences was that they were unavoidable, and then some function or interpretation was added onto that.

I approached the concept of schizophrenia, at first cautiously. I came to the conclusion that if there was something rational interpreted from schizoophrenia, it was that schizophrenia was a psychological reality for the patient. Which was reasonable enough. On one level, it was automatic to accept this, on another level it was profoundly difficult. And the patients' symptoms were themselves difficult.

The conclusion was, on some level, if a

schiizophrenic's mind was real, and performing functions, then it was a kind of multi-mind. Not a split-personality, but a mishmash of psychological influences. The difficulty for the schizophrenic is that some of these 'voices' these symptoms, did not automatically integrate with the patient's own mind and personality.

It was easy to psychologize, and assume that this interpretation was merely an experience of therapy, or an experience of 'understanding the patient'. But more directly, or honestly, it was an insight into the multi-mind. Not the split-personality, but the community of identity. Schizophrenia was in some sense, real, because, relative to the symptoms, the patient's identity was conflicted, and the conflict was the result of real things, however subtle or unhealthy.

True, this was against traditional therapy --- against the minds of the true believers --- but it was also the only hope of addressing the real mind of the schizophrenic. Whether these thoughts the schizophrenic had originated outside, and whether the schizophrenic participated in some dissipated although not usually experienced 'common' reality were therefore open questions.

The nature of the multi-mind resolved them. For the un-integrated components of the mind were always, at least, mental components in the sense that they were expressed. In the same way that a spiritual magician could make people appear in front of him, the schizo-phrenic could make these dysfunctional thoughts appear in front of their own mind. Thus, like the magician aims to integrate real people, the schizophrenic aims to integrate, and be a magician of his own mind. So, the first factor of the multi-mind was that the thoughts of the schizophrenic had at least one mental attribute. And the mental attribute is what is being expressed to the client (by his mind).

A second factor was a factor univer-sally perceived by schizophrenic, which is the quality of a 'common reality' or 'community experience' of the mental events. My advice here was not to 'shrink' the schizophrenic deeper into analysis (which seems like a head-ache of minmalism), but instead, for the client to adopt the voices from the larger world, into his own mind. And, by this process, to accept that the world is in effect his own mind. That what he knows of the world, insofar as it in-volves his thinking and interpretation, is his mind. That what he has trouble hearing is things outside his mind.

Thirdly, when the community of voices can be seen as belonging only within his mind, he will recognize that most of those voices are himself, and some of the other voices are just opinions and judgments which are less impor-tant than his own voice, and a third thing is the madness which only comes from other people, and a fourth thing is the neutral but rational objects of experience.

Thus, working backwards, we can see that schizoophrenia results from thinking that objects are mad, from thinking that oneself is mad, from being confused by opinions and judgments, from losing or not developing one's own character, and from attaching one's interior thoughts to the objects of the exterior.

Brokenality

Recently I thought of a fourth concept of psychology inspired by the earlier three. It is a rebellious concept, and not likely to be accepted by mainstream psychologists. In fact, it runs against the instincts of therapists. (On the other hand, it is not like psychologists have never seen radical concepts).

Brokenality is about moving beyond traditional concepts of functionality and dysfunction. Instead of saying 'The patient's condition must improve, or else!' or 'If it's not broken don't fix it' instead, we say 'Broken things are the only departure point for fixing anything!'

But it is important to add that this is an intellectual attitude that is all about new departures. The client isn't supposed to think that they are supposed to feel ill, or that it was inevitable that they became hurt. Rather, they are mean to feel that everything they do for recovery corresponds to that time in their life when they felt just as good, an equal time before the illness, which has already happened.

Every time we recover, we join in that part of ourselves that came before the illness, and we also make a free exploration into the great creative unknown which happens after illness. Thus, recovery is a natural process. It is about accepting that something happened, and it's not everything, and a large part of life lies beyond illness. As soon as we're broken we've realized we're broken, and as soon as we've realized we're broken, we've moved beyond being broken.

The boredom, and consciousness, of being broken is what makes us not broken. As soon as we accept that we're broken, we've moved into a new kind of toughness, and a new kind of optimism. It is only those who do not realize the advantages and limitations of illness who do not recover, because the only reason to be unfair is to gain an advantage. Therefore, nothing is absolutely unfair. At the very least, we've been granted an opportunity.

What is most important?

What are the three most important things in life?

1. Resources like air to breathe, food, clothing, shelter, the right temperature, plumbing, electricity…

2. Happiness. People don't think life is very good without some degree of happiness.

3. Meaning. Even if people are happy, they start to feel weird if there is not purpose or intellectual meaning, or some form of explanation in life. Forms of meaning vary somewhat because different people feel different things are important in part because they gain advantages from different things / opportunities. However, there is some evidence that forms of meaning are somewhat bound together, and some forms of meaning such as reading and writing and art are fairly universal. We can add to this some aspects of mathematics and how the mind works as long as it is understood that different people have different motivations and may be very different emotionally or in terms of how they explain their own life to others. The modal inflection of how-to-explain-to-others and degree of meaning in someone's life may be more important than how actually different someone is.

Synesthesia and Psychology

Perhaps it is due to fear that particular people, such as sons and daughters of divorced parents, such as myself, lose their taste for complex flavors, and consequently lose their complete sense of reality, resulting in illnesses such as depersonalization and schizophrenia.

Before every impression is fully-formed is a stage in which one may have a negative impression. It is difficult to overcome this mistake. Therefore, to overt the worst conclusions, all impressions should be positive, or concealed in sophistication or some other guise, which permits us to derive positive benefit from the material. One, the positive view, is the view of masters and children. The other, the sophisticated view, is the view of Plato's Academy. With licenses like these, history pivots on nothing more than applications.

When people learn to cope with coping, they gain happiness.

When people express what they dislike, they become aliens.

It's possible masturbation comes about through some type of asexual reproduction, like a posteriori information propogation.

Curious people find that insensitive food creates sensitivity, by stimulating curiosity. People who are not curious find that sensitive food promotes insensitivity, by stimulating disgust. It is senses like these that originated the concept of many-worlds, and we separate metaphysical theories from human complexity at the expense of our own understanding, if not the realizations of those forms of complexity. The reality in the sense of being separated is not differentiated, although it could easily embody unrelated things of equal complexity.

A Theory of Thought: Happiness is an exaggeration of a different feeling, which is the pinching feeling of having criteria for intelligence. Without a criteria, the happiness escapes. Without happiness, the thought is not great. A thought begins with a pinch, becomes intelligent, then becomes happy, then becomes great.

What is commonly meant by meaning defers to ultimate meaning, unless the ultimate meaning fails. Therefore, one should not defer to common meaning, unless the commonplace is itself ultimate. Therefore, there is a choice between two logics: failure and the ultimate. But what is meant by the ultimate is not just any ultimate. It begins with the good of the individual, and is elaborated through reference to systems, modes, and values.

Ultimate variation begins with the motive for change.

It is possible to remember pain that was not conscious the first time: pain-as-information which threatens to emerge, just as other information threatens to submerge in fantasies.

The things that can be simulated in the mind resemble exactly the substances of which the mind is composed. Out of the materialism of the mind, we can suppose there are materials that are not of the mind, and yet related to the mind!

Indeed, the sensibility of the mind appears to be a fifth thing: beyond mind, reason, object, and its shadow.

Children benefit from hearing elementary ideas that concern a conscious learning process. Adults benefit by a variety of approaches, including stimulation & emphasis, core concepts, and unique ideas.

General feelings communicate --- specific feelings are obvious.

Each person is confronting his or her own deepest problems. This explains the emotional difficulty some people have.

Passive mania is genius bottled up and waiting to be born! But when passive mania is expressed, it does not always take the form of manic-depression. There are various ways of coping with genius, just as there are various ways of coping with illness.

People who are racially or denominatively prejudiced are trying to raise their own sensory awareness. It is similar to identifying with pain. Prejudice also occurs in response to sensory cues which subject individuals associate with depersonalization or inhumanity.

Among the most suppressed theories in psychology: Aggression is correlated with excitement. Criminals may be thrill-seekers. Sexuality is correlated with victimization. Therefore, sexy people are not always functional people. Genius is correlated with madness, therefore intelligence is not strictly correlated with functionality. Stupid people (people with 90 - 100 IQ) tend to be basically functional, although often they fault their IQ in spite of this.

Sick people can still be greedy. This explains a lot about the human problem of evil. People have limited opportunities to develop the worst problems. Then most people become ill, and illness is blamed for an array of sins. People who stay well are considered blessed, and put on a plateau where they are expected to do nothing. By doing nothing, these blessed people remain blameless and good, while the remainder are sick and evil. However, for the evil people there is the excuse that illness is to blame. When good, innocent people become evil, it is declared a social ailment, a degree higher than the sickness of evil. What every moral psychologist wants to declare is that 'society was already sick', when in fact it is the psychology of evil that is sick, and physical sickness itself is no more than coincidental, or perhaps sometimes, convenient. In sum, human evil might be blamed on sickness, the inability to recover, and the worshipping of blameless idols.

The fault of science appears to be a generic psychological mistake: the idea that science is good simply because the scientific mind is good, when in reality any good mind has good results, with or without science.

People who construct their brains are the intermediate type of intelligence. The lowest type succeeds but rarely to construct anything intellectual. The highest type has moved beyond construction to the experiencing of what things really are: mathematics, wisdom, conversations, character, experience. In fact, the experiencing of the brain can lead to this form of intelligence, but requires at least the upper end of intermediate intelligence. While great intelligence first happens by fate, the determination of fate actually occurs by commitment.

On some level, the mentally weak may be attempting to make examples of themselves. There is perhaps nothing fundamentally wrong with setting an example, but without a capacity to set a real standard of what the example means, without the authority that comes with education or happiness, these examples fail to demonstrate anything that they set out to do. Perhaps ordinary people are merely successful at making examples, and this is what distinguishes them from those who are handicapped. But examples of what? What if the successful cases were examples of cruel evolutionary advantages, while the less successful examples served to illustrate dire premonitions? The strength at this point is once again the strength of example.

Suicide (when it occurs) is not just a result of bad feelings, but looking the wrong way, and then being put inside a suicidal category. This is especially true of *repeated suicide attempts*. One should never want a suicidal norm, but that is what is created by this false and superficial attitude. Under this mentality, those who don't commit suicide are those who never reach that level of self-disrespect, or that level of desire for peeling away the layers of authority.

When someone thinks that someone is emotionally hurt, this could mean that things are acceptable. It could also mean that there are large questions, and it could mean that the problem is more serious than assumed. The compound of 'big question - suffering - acceptable' is often not what we think emotionally. We often assume others feel better than us, and put them on a plateau. But, in fact, they have the same feelings we have when we are not asking questions about others' emotions.

What Wisdom Do I Have That Others Don't?:

In the wisdom department, I know that it is usually the very beginning of a thought process that can lead someone down the wrong path. A lot of people don't seem to question their assumptions, or feel satisfied accepting some degree of imperfection in their past. Even though perfectionism runs the risk of stress and madness, its one of the best ways to pursue the best life.

Once we accept perfectionism, many choices are more arbitrary than we think. The stress we bear from day to day is sometimes an arbitrary choice based on what we merely ASSUME is appropriate. We can feel better by training ourselves to be patient, and make slow turns towards a healthier mentality. For example, it is possible to become vegetarian, to avoid depression, or to be more intellectual. However, these options imply changing more than one thing about one's life simultaneously.

At the root of it, what inspires us is the least flexible thing. If we can change what inspires us, we have the ability to change everything about ourselves.

Collectively, these 'secrets' are very powerful for creating change in one's life.

Advanced Concept of Development

Organization of levels is something of a difficult task, since many beings see themselves in different ways.

I have already given the organization of 'the levels of path' in the following form: (1) Brute Survival. (2) Organized Warfare. (3) Economic Value. (4) Intellectual Meaning.

That is more of a historical perspective than an objective view.

An initial guide to objective levels may be found by the following organization:

1. The Trivial. Mere opinions. Arbitrary judgments. Confusion. Lack of reality. Requires a basic paradigm and no work.

2. The Real. That which makes an impression, and little more. That which can be counted on. The conventional. The predictable. The things that do not always require knowledge. Requires a basic paradigm and work.

3. The Dimensional. The conceptual and meaningful. That which understands the real. It requires an advanced paradigm AND work.

4. The Ideal. That which has extended beyond reality into hyper-reality and fantasy. That which no longer requires a conventional stan-

dard. That which requires an advanced paradigm, but no work.

We can see from these four fundamental levels THAT leveling involves advancement under two paradigms: (1) Actualization, and (2) Meaning. Moving beyond actualized meaning would mean extending beyond the first MAJOR quadra of levels. Doing so reliably would not be easy, but may be possible.

Infantile Psychology

Infants, it is known, have a lot of care for their
mothers.

Much of the infant's immediate life has to do
with his or her dependence on the mother.

The infant may also learn a lot from the
mother's and father's response to him or her,
and the initial experiences in the hospital
or wherever else the infant is born.

Indeed, the child's early experiences are exaggerated. Depending on what senses are avail-
able to the child, the infant may learn
considerably, or else not as much as average.

The earliest experiences are the moments in
which the infant reaches the first inclinations
towards whatever wisdom or insight
that will be had later in life.

This first insight has two parts: (1) The child's
unhindered perceptions about the world,
whether pleasant or unpleasant,
whether insightful, or recoiling, etc. and (2)
The permission granted throughout later life to
trust these perceptions and enjoy
or critique existence.

The first major opportunity for the infant may
be to avoid suffering, and if this is not successful the world becomes a treacherous place, full
of shadows and phantoms.

The second opportunity is to be wise, and this is on the basis of the extent to which the infant's first insights can blossom. That is, whether the infant was confused or not. How fresh in memory, how free of narcotics was the mother, etc.

The third opportunity is to be critical, which is something that tends to happen to a greater extent if the child is unhappy, but also when the child is supported by the environment.

Thus, the Happy, Wise, and Petulent children are the three archetypes that emerge. And their semiforms are respetively the Funny, Intelligent, and Perceptive.

The best to emerge from a bad life is the perceptive child, while the best to emerge from a good life is the happy child. In that way, there is some compensation for the pains of life.

Mainstream Psychology

Mainstream psychology has a reputation for a certain nimble, affable attitude which makes its subjects more appealing to a popular audience. This form of psychology is virtually unique for its 1-to-1 relevance to the audience, and its immediate applicability in the personal and interpersonal world of its audience.

Mainstream psychology is often summarized in individual 'grand theses', often combining words such as 'individual (adj.)', 'passivity / aggression / intelligence / schizophrenia / depression', 'improves / spirals out of control', 'under some [stated] conditions'. The conditions can be stated to be a byproduct of further factors such as 'de-socialization / de-sensitization / stimulation / group settings'. Some bizarre theses seem to hold under the conditions of certain illnesses, or under bizarre stimulus. Thus, some of the conditions may have results only under 'over-exposure / with high intensity' or 'if the client is sensitive to the stimulus'.

Thus, mainstream psychology can be mapped as follows:

1. Sensitive?
2. Exposed?
3. Bizarre?
4. Social psychology?
5. Stimulus? De-sensitized or de-socialized?
6. Condition?

7. Chronic?
8. Depressed?
9. Dysfunctional?
10. Intelligent (specific sensitivity)?
11. Passive / aggressive (hidden symptoms)?

For example,

A. Bee-sting. Physical sensitivity. Requires physical treatment or
tolerance.
B. Allergy to yogurt. Sensitivity with a condition. May affect
certain social situations.
C. Person is behaving bizarrely because they are not wearing any
clothes. Person may have dementia or excessive promiscuity.
Problem needs to be solved immediately.
D. Person feels social anxiety. Person is otherwise mentally
healthy. Condition which applies in all social situations.
E. Person has a concealed megalomania. This is social
psychology that applies only in certain social situations.
F. Person is feeling discomfort in the office. This may be a
product of a physical or mental condition.
G. Person is feeling very alert. The person may be drugged or
experiencing psychosis or exaggerated emotions.
H. Person doesn't show up at the appointment. Person may be

disorganized, forgetful, or have a physical impairment.

I. Person's condition doesn't improve. The condition may be
habitual, chronic, fatal, or in some other way serious.

J. Person is dysfunctional and blames their mood. Person may be
depressed.

K. Person doesn't handle social situations very well. Person may
be emotionally immature, abused, schizophrenic, or
developmentally abnormal (high I.Q.).

L. Person is especially complex on one issue. Person may simply
have special knowledge in this area (high I.Q.).

M. Person is especially un-forthcoming on one particular topic in
her life. Person may have suppressed memories.

Forms of Psychic Prediction

Psychic prediction may take several basic forms.

First I will describe the most basic types of prediction.

First of all, the most basic type is 0-dimensional prediction. This consists of predicting what has already occurred, that is, predicting the types of things that have already happened. A second degree of this is had by predicting things that are similar to those things that have happened. For our purposes, this can be called simple generalization. *If Henrick usually wants to play games, perhaps he wants to play games now.* This is the first dimension of prediction, and it is the type that gains most easily by probabilistic inductions. This method is also called specialized prediction when it is applied to specialized modes of behavior. For example, we can predict that a Matisse will sell high compared to an unknown artist. We know that popular items in an auction sell high, whereas unpopular items might not sell at all. Therefore, there is an exponential relationship for example, between selling a Matisse, and selling a Matisse at an auction. These kinds of things can be predicted by studying the specific character of the modalities and events involved in a given situation. However, if an event is instead informal or contrived, this lends an aspect of unpredictability. The predictions only work when all of the

prior conditions are met, and become less predictable with every difference from the previous cases. Therefore, differences can be used
to predict differences, as another type of specialized prediction. It may help to predict trick-
ery or confusion ('likely outcomes'), rather
than predicting a specific event. It should be
accepted that some conditions and choices are
arbitrary. *Because we do not know if conditions
will be met to satisfaction, we know that some
events are arbitrary.* If the conditions are one
half different, then prediction requires a strong
degree of formalism, however that is calcu-
lated. It involves, in effect, exceeding expecta-
tions, or coming across an event that happened
just in the same way, but as if by chance. This
is one reason that scientists have been known
to require the reproduction of *laboratory conditions*, even with highly predictable phenomena. Thus, specialized predictions have some
limitations.

The next type is delineative or elaborative prediction. What it consists of is a generalization
modified by additional imagination about the
significance of the factors involved. This type
of prediction can be called variablistic, because
it often functions by applying a generalization
to a deduction about a variable. *If elephants
are painted red, perhaps it is a sight for sore
eyes*, etc. One form of this is prediction
through emergence. This is not necessarily a
linear prediction because it essentially doesn't
predict based on existing data. Nor does it predict based on known exterior data. Instead, it
involves a conclusion that *something is missing*

from the data. Logical conclusions are drawn so that we can make major systemic conclusions about what the data means. The new theory appears *as if from thin air*. This is similar to the emergence of Darwinism, or the genetic explanation of reproduction. What determines the success of these theories is their relative importance, not necessarily the lack of any alternative. It is the importance of the theory---- its *emergence*----which drives the prediction. (Many theories from social science involve emergent theories, such as socialism and capitalism. Instead of acting as a formal constraint, they often expand the way that the conditions function. In this case, the explanation is not erroneous, but instead, serves as a *new rational mode of explanation*).

A third type is contingent or categorical prediction. If something is the case, then we can predict that the things that rely upon this first condition are modified when that category is modified. This form of prediction works better for predicting quality differences than actually-different conditions. However, if multiple qualities are absent, predictions can be made about the alternatives. *If there is no snow, it can be predicted that it is not cold, or there is a shortage of water, for instance. If it is not cold, one can predict that it is arid or moist. If there is a shortage of water, one can predict that it is dry, or there is a high tolerance for water.* This can also take the form of complex categorization. Attaching variables to a given object means that predicting the outcome for the main object affects the outcome of some, if not all, of the variables. For example, '*if we do something extreme, the change might be observable. Otherwise, it is an abstract or unmeasurable form of extremity. We must have some means of observation, or we can usually conclude that the effects are not extreme. Or we can adopt an irrational view*'.

A fourth type of prediction is coherent prediction. This is also called synergism or epiphany. The simplest form of coherent prediction occurs by the exclusion of all but one unlikely option. *Hella spent a hot day in the desert, and she was outdoors, and walked several miles, time passed and she didn't expire: she must have brought something to drink with her.* A more complex form occurs by qualifying what it means to make a given combination. *People who have complicit sex are always lovers. Therefore, if two people have sex, it might be complicit, and they might be lovers. Or, something is complicit between two people. If it is sex, they are lovers.* This can even involve highly complex phenomena. For example: *Joe defines himself as an editor, but he works as an economist. In some way he is doing economic editing.* This is the beginning of a genuinely psychic method. Attaching judgments of fully embraced variables can be a meaningful way of reaching for epiphanies. For example, what 'definitely IS something' about a given thing? Then apply that condition to factors like responsibility, organization, and predictability. An exception to this is so-called 'black swans'. In that case, one must predict the rationale which *makes* something a black swan. The rule in that case is that things are either unreasonable, reasonable, without purpose, or serving a prescribed function. A method for solving black swans involves corroboration or defaulting. This occurs when there is no better explanation remaining for a given thing. *Well, we know that such-and-such a creature has eyes based on the related species, but nothing about the creature looks exactly like eyes. The eyes must be these spots on its back. Otherwise its blind.* Or, black swans could exist, as long as we know that color serves no inherent function.

Now for more genuine psychic predictions:

A second genuine form of psychic prediction involves using a posteriori reasoning on a 0-dimensional prediction. For example, *if we know that some events are arbitrary, then we can derive that we don't know if some conditions will be met to satisfaction. If we know Henrick wants to play games now, we can predict that he usually wants to play games.* This form of prediction often involves deducing the types of statements that lead to a particular line of reasoning: that is, *predicting a rationale.* Many psychics are familiar with this way of phrasing deductions.

A third form of genuine psychic prediction involves determination based on unstated facts. Since everyone thinks about the opposite of what they say, at least unconsciously, combining multiple opposite terms for terms that have been stated as someone's opinion, or as the definition of a motive or interest for the person or organization, will give information about the genuine motivations, or else the looming unknowns in the life of the person or organization. For example, if someone states that the first thing on their mind is their motorcycle, and the second thing on their mind is their manhood, then you can predict that they're concerned about meeting someone else on a motorcycle.

A fourth form of genuine psychic prediction involves categorical relationships. One can ask or predict 'what is someone's usual mode of relation with the world?' Then one can predict that they use that mode of relation with their perceived opposites. For example, an artist who expresses that the thing on his mind is cars can be predicted '*not to buy a painting of a car, instead you'll make it yourself*' (the concealed opposition is between the artist who makes art, and his opposite, the buyer of the art. The opposite of making a painting of a car is buying a painting of a car). Similarly, if a business expresses itself as aggressive and competitive, but you think they're liars, you can predict they'll have contradictory marketing ('competing truths', since their mode of relation is competition, and their opposite is the truth).

A fifth form of genuine psychic prediction: take any number of factors describing a current event or situation you're in, and reverse the factors that are different from the subject. This can be used to predict how someone is feeling, or what their core motivation are. For example, an artist is at a business convention. So they're feeling unconventional, and they feel like making art, since that is not a different motive from business. Or, a philosophy society is at an art gallery. So, it thinks its popular art ('society' does not conflict with 'gallery'), and it thinks its un-philosophical art, or tries to make connections between art and philosophy ('philosophy' is different from 'art' or it can be debated). Other conclusions might be that they think art is trying to commercialize philosophy, that philosophy ought to involve graphics, or to view art or philosophy as a socialist movement.

Those are the eight categories of prediction that I have determined. I hope this writing may be considered useful to my readers on this most often unrealized subject.

Harmonizing

There is much confusion about the concept of harmonization. It has been seen as central to functional psychology for a long time. However, its root causes, and the means of sustaining it have been (for some) by turns difficult or obscure.

Harmonizing, which is the process of reaching harmonization, comes about through a practical focus on positive thinking, both to avoid disaster, and to promote valuable mentalistic vibes.

Harmonization becomes more difficult for those who are brain-damaged, or for some other reason cannot find genuine mental stimulation. The ability to stimulate the mind is what separates so-called 'ordinary' people from those who are considered abnormal. Further traits such as ethical conduct, professional qualifications, fatherliness or motherliness, etc. seperate further the functional types, but for dysfunctional people some or all of these additional traits may often be impossible.

Harmonization becomes the exclusive bridge between functional and dysfunctional people, and it is by no means an easy bridge to cross, as the positive elements of harmony are held almost exclusively by functional people.

A key element to understand is that harmonizing involves ignoring and eliminating harmful

vibes, which can be detected and
criticized by those with intellectual sensitivity.
The truly functional people tend to be high intellectual performers, or at least high social
performers.

On the converse, ignoring harmful vibes has
been critiqued as a 'following-the-herd' mentality, but so long as mental stimulation
is a desirable end in itself, some degree of con-
formism is largely unavoidable, and can even
inspire envy.

Intellectual sensitivity and higher cognitive
traits become the defense against invasive
negative behaviors that could compromise the
culture and chemistry of such close-knit net-
works of reward and response.

The reward, some say it is a lofty one, is to be
mentally constructive by providing a culture
for the higher mental ambitions of groups of
individuals. Because groups tend to have
higher social functions than individuals, there
is an advantage in giving preference to group
function over individual function.

On the other hand, ignoring individual function
may prohibit creativity if the focus is no longer
on genuine individual accomplishment. Thus,
the model must be accepted on a chemical
level of mutual exchange before harmonization
works for individuals.

It is then likely that the system of harmonization is keyed into patterns that only emerge

with sexual or narcotic stimulus.

So, while harmony works for society, it is superficial in the sense that it has no one individual's interest in mind independent of the overall social function.

On the other hand, it is geared towards the immediate chemical achievement of every individual in the context of any existing context of limitations.

Harmony thus involves such things as simple awareness, the desire for stimulus, and social priorities which are assumed to be the honest traits of humans as individuals when they seek to fulfill non-negativist priorities.

Individuation

INSPIRATION --- At first, the individual
(subject) is surrounded
by talented people, often people who play music instruments.
Their talent is explained by the fact that they have already
individuated. This is also the time when the person first hears the
word 'individual'.

THE LIE --- The person sees that there is something wrong with
the world. The person struggles and is taken down by a
psychological or physical condition of some type. He or she hears
the word 'individuation' if it is psychological, or 'habit' /
'habitation' / 'habituation' if it is physical. The physical response
leads to questions such as, is it worth it to spend time, is life worth
it, is the physical world inspiring, etc. It cannot be argued that
both worlds are equally interesting, so the physical answer may
involve some sort of artificial death or histori-cal lapse into the
psychological condition. In effect, the physical model becomes the
background.

THEORY AND PROOF --- The individual explores creativity or
whatever else he or she feels like doing. The result is a theory
(what he or she is doing) and confirmation (proof of the theory),
not to be confused with the later stage.

IMMERSION OR DENIAL ---- As life be-comes more like a
mental construct that responds to some of the person's thoughts
(e.g. the person gets some of what is wanted), either the person

immerses him or herself in pleasures, or he or
she denies him or
herself some of the pleasures. The result is two
different
personalities, one finding unreality in the
physical body, and the
other finding unreality in the mind.
CONFORMATION --- The theory, whether it
is flesh or mind,
becomes all-important, and the persons' beliefs
as they become
more sophisticated are also confirmed or supported.
ELEVATION - THE KISS ---- Rewards become immaterial or
else confirm one's habituation in the world.
One enters 'the psychological cocoon'.

Mnemosis

Mnemosis, or recovery of memories, is a technique that has fallen out of fashion in psychology. Psychologists have discovered that patients are dishonest, temperamental, or just
can't get themselves to remember everything.

Nonetheless, confrontation with past events is
an important process in therapy, and takes
place even if it is not frankly acknowledged.
And, often the therapist is aware of this.

The process may vary somewhat, but it is usually in the following form:

1. The therapist asks the patient polite questions (how he or she is feeling, what is something that matters to them, where have they traveled to, etc.)

2. The therapist asks the patient to explain something in their life that is important to them, such as a memory that they think of fondly, or some recent experience that has troubled them.

3. Instead of immediately analyzing what the trouble or significance means, the therapist asks the person what the thing, event, significance, etc. means to the patient.

4. Through internally analyzing what the patient interprets from the experience, the therapist begins to understand the patient.

5. The therapist can develop a network of associations about thepatient by asking more questions, and delving deeper into the patient's past experiences and associations.

6. Finally, through guidance from the therapist, the patient is led into an understanding of what is most important to them.

7. If what seems most important is something harmful or dangerous, the therapist can warn the patient that there is something harmful or dangerous lurking in their psyche.

Gestalt Theory

Take a value and find out that it's true, and theoretically you've found what is known as a 'gestalt' or deep psychological truism.

For example, if authentic life is happy, and happiness is always symbolized by the color 'yellow', then we can say 'life is yellow' is a gestalt. Even if it isn't 100% true, it is a truism because its supposed to be true.

Similarly, we can say 'systems live in trees' if all systems come from linear structures which are called trees.

Brain Repair and "the Poodle Effect"

This is something I have noticed that is very
important, so I will
mention it first.

People are often set off course by the appear-
ance of poodles!
Seriously!

They think their brain is composed like a poodle, and then they
have to undo the effect!

Until they learn to squash in these exaggerated
'puffs' of their
brain, there is no hope of recovering mental
function.

This effect is even more extreme on the brain
than the
hyper-activity resulting from sugar, only the
effect is opposite.

Overcoming the poodle effect could almost be
called the first
stage towards mental functionality. But we
should ultimately
avoid expressions like 'ascendent brain' as
these may have
similar effects, albeit not as extreme as the
poodle.

I have cured at least one person's thoughtless-
ness by mentioning

this problem!

Ignorance-Denial:

Are you imagining the obvious when you need
to?

Are your eyes black and you have never
thought they could be
like charcoal, even in passing?

This may be a sign of excessive mental re-
straint.

Instead, consider the obvious, and reject it if
you like.
The process can be oft-repeated.

Insights

The opti-mystics thought wine was blood and wasn't for drinking. The pessi-mystics thought wine was poison and drunk it up.

I have found those accepting illusions are those forgiving god, whereas pleasure is simply the pursuit of genius.

Surely one doesn't need a lifetime for every lesson! Most life-lessons seem to amount to this.

'Practical' is the most ideal word in a higher language.

Things are as valuable as they are,
But they are not as valuable as we assume!

When we have the best senses, there is no pain.
We have to balance who we are relative to what we observe, that's what creates pain.

Humans are infinitely sensitive, but not absolutely.

Faith in pain is meaningless.

I think possibly each life has a different meta-physical existence, and sometimes these meta-physical existences are held in common with other people When they are held in common with other people, then they have a political reality, or an economic reality, or a divine reality, etc. Different labels might apply in different 'universes' although some of the universes are really earlier or later variations of other universes, and sometimes even things like 'Time' might exist in one universe but not in another. The conditions of the universe depend both on the big and the small, and people can think that small or big things matter almost arbitrarily, deciding how life is determined for themselves (if they have authority), and for something else outside themselves if they do not have authority. And this intuition might only apply to some small aspect of the real reality.

Can Jung's Archetypes be Falsified?

Principles from Gestalt Theory have some appeal, such as the idea that 'all systems are up a tree' because a linear structure prefigures many system structures. Or, the idea that 'nature is yellow' if yellow represents happiness, and happiness is optimal, and nature is ideally optimal. These ideas are idealistic to be sure, but higher cognition does not necessarily eliminate idealistic notions, and may often gain usefulness by placing demands on them.

There is a big difference between Jung's archetypes conceived in an obvious sense, say, interpolated with media images or memes, and Jung's archetypes seen in great depth. I think the moral of the archetypes is that (1) They or incoherent, because one image is not compatible with another, etc. or (2) They are coherent, but only insofar as they meet the criteria of coherency. With this understanding, it is possible to examine the archetypes carefully and extract a psychological lesson focusing on voluntary self-development. I think this is the core lesson that Jung meant to protract.

The Problem With Therapy

Therapy sometimes takes the form of the ego.

A good friend said that sometimes the ego takes the form of problem-solving.

But, problem-solving contains the word <u>problem</u>.

This seems to assume that solutions are mere problems and that some people don't <u>have</u> a problem. Some people are just coping.

This seems to express a fundamental barrier: a way to psychology is too intrusive.

Perhaps we should accept the paradigmatic in every individual. Otherwise, we are creating problems.

Should we create problems? If not, we should accept the fundamentals of individualism.

Things You Can't Psychologize

"Sometimes I think the universe is just being efficient".

I asked my imaginary patient to explain this a little more, and he said,

"You need to remember that when I masturbate, I don't masturbate about therapy. But I'm a good person."

Clearly this guy knew what he was talking about.

It was not an unconscious admission.

Should I take him at his word?

Was he an unwilling psychopath?

In short, should I judge him as good or bad?

Clearly he wanted me to partake of the fruit of good and evil.

But could he offer such fruit?

Based on this experience, I wanted to conclude that analysis may have a psychological dead-end.

Then the patient said to me:

"Sometimes I pray that the smokers would go away."

The instinct of the therapist is to say this person is being difficult.

Does the patient want the smokers to die?

But it turns out, the patient doesn't want the smokers to die, he just wants them to go away.

Is this a mental problem, or a physical one?

Is the patient confused?

In what case is the prayer successful?

When the patient can 'cope' with the smokers, or when the smokers actually go away?

Many people would side with the patient on this one.

The patient is not confused, he is just facing a difficult situation.

But then, what is wrong with having a difficult problem?

And, is being a difficult person really the answer to the conflict the person is having?

At this point, it seems that it is the therapist that needs therapy.

The therapist shouldn't recommend that the person starts smoking!

The therapist shouldn't recommend that he become friends with the smokers and pick up the habit!

The therapist should just hope that the prayer is realized, and the smokers go away!

It is almost as if the therapist is being the difficult person!

Nathan Coppedge

OTHER TEXTS BY THE AUTHOR:

The Dimensional Psychologist's Toolkit

Psychological Knowledge

Psychic Prediction Techniques

ARTICLES

Applicationist Psychology. Academia

Functional Psychology. Academia

On Negativity. Academia

Semantics of Psychology. Academia

NATHAN COPPEDGE is the author of numerous books on psychology, including titles on child development, mental-health focus, and traditional psychology. The present work is a compilation of previous writings including those included in Systems Theory, a larger work by the same author.

www.ingramcontent.com/pod-product-compliance
Lightning Source LLC
Chambersburg PA
CBHW071251280526
45788CB00004B/1668